NATIONAL GEOGRAPHIC
READING EXPEDITIONS®

PLANET PATROL

Outback Adventure

By Rebecca L. Johnson

Illustrated by Tom Newsom

PICTURE CREDITS
4 (top) © Tom Newsom; 6 (left to right)
© Ingram Publishing/Alamy, © Robert Harding
Picture Library Ltd/Alamy; 7 Mapping
Specialists, Ltd.; 64 © D. Robert and Lorri
Franz/Corbis.

Produced through the worldwide resources of
the National Geographic Society, John M. Fahey,
Jr., President and Chief Executive Officer;
Gilbert M. Grosvenor, Chairman of the Board;
Nina D. Hoffman, Executive Vice President and
President, Books and Education Publishing
Group.

**PREPARED BY NATIONAL GEOGRAPHIC
SCHOOL PUBLISHING**
Ericka Markman, Senior Vice President and
President, Children's Books and Education
Publishing Group; Steve Mico, Senior Vice
President, Publisher, Editorial Director; Francis
Downey, Executive Editor; Richard Easby,
Editorial Manager; Bea Jackson, Director of
Design; Cynthia Olson, Art Director; Margaret
Sidlosky, Director of Illustrations; Matt
Wascavage, Manager of Publishing Services;
Lisa Pergolizzi, Sean Philpotts, Production
Managers, Ted Tucker, Production Specialist.

MANUFACTURING AND QUALITY CONTROL
Christopher A. Liedel, Chief Financial Officer;
Phillip L. Schlosser, Director; Clifton M. Brown,
Manager.

EDITORS
Barbara Seeber, Mary Anne Wengel

BOOK DEVELOPMENT
Morrison BookWorks LLC

BOOK DESIGN
Steven Curtis Design

ART DIRECTION
Dan Banks, Project Design Company

Published by the National Geographic Society
1145 17th Street, N.W.
Washington, D.C. 20036-4688

ISBN: 0-7922-5855-X

3 4 5 6 7 8 9 10 11   20 19 18 17 16 15 14

Contents

Into the Outback

Dr. Bender finished reading the last application from the stack on his desk. Hundreds had arrived in response to the advertisement he'd posted last month. Dr. Bender set four applications off to one side. By the end of the day, Drew, Amy, Troy, and Janice would know they'd be the chosen interns. Soon they would be on their way to the Australian outback!

**Drew Payton
age 13
New Brighton,
Pennsylvania**
I've always loved learning about Australian animals. To see a kangaroo—or a bilby—in the wild would be fantastic!

**Amy Chang
age 12
Portland, Oregon**
Camping and hiking are two things I love to do. I think I'd be good to have around in any camp—even one in a desert.

4

Attention Young Explorers!

EcoAware is dedicated to promoting science and environmental awareness around the world. We want to involve young people in our research projects. EcoAware will give four students, ages 11 to 13, a chance to work with Dr. Duncan Woollera in South Australia's arid outback for one month. Dr. Woollera studies bilbies, small marsupials that are being reintroduced into areas where they have become extinct. If you are interested, fill out the application and send it to Dr. Alan Bender at EcoAware.

**Troy Ramirez
age 11
Rock Island, Illinois**
I live along the Mississippi River, so water is part of my life. I think it would be really amazing to experience a desert.

**Janice Nielson
age 13
Tucson, Arizona**
I want to know how the plants and animals in the outback compare to those in the Sonoran Desert, which is almost in my backyard.

The Australian Outback

After the interns accepted their assignment, Dr. Bender e-mailed this fact sheet about Australia to them.

The Outback

Australia is the only country in the world that is also a continent. Australia is big. It is the seventh largest country in the world. But it has a small population. Only about 20 million people live there.

Animals in the outback have adapted to survive with very little water. Many are nocturnal. This means they sleep during the day and are active at night.

The outback is mostly desert. It is located in the middle of the country. Most people don't live in the outback because it is hot and dry. The land is flat and rocky. Not much vegetation grows there.

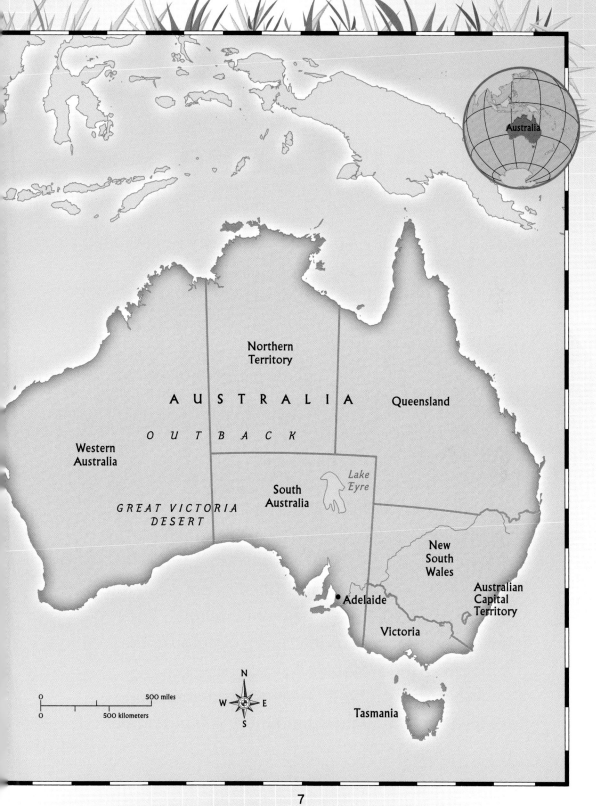

Australia

Northern
Territory

A U S T R A L I A

Queensland

O U T B A C K

Western
Australia

Lake
Eyre

South
Australia

GREAT VICTORIA
DESERT

New
South
Wales

Australian
Capital
Territory

• Adelaide

Victoria

0   500 miles

N

0   500 kilometers

W   E

S

Tasmania

CHAPTER 1

Arid Zone

"Well, they sure are cute," Amy remarked. She was looking at a picture in the book she'd brought along to read on the flight.

"What's cute?" Troy asked. He was sitting in the seat next to her.

"Bilbies—the little animals we're going to be studying with Dr. Woollera," she replied, showing him the picture. "They look a bit like rabbits with pointy noses."

"Yes, they do," Dr. Bender chimed in. He was sitting across the aisle of the plane. "I once read somewhere that bilbies are the Australian version of the Easter bunny."

"You know," Drew said, "they're not related to rabbits at all. They're a type of marsupial. They have a pouch for carrying their young, just like kangaroos and wombats."

"What's a wombat?" Janice asked, munching the peanuts the flight attendant was handing out.

"It's another kind of marsupial," Drew replied. "If we're lucky, we might see some wombats where we're going."

"Bilbies? Wombats?" Janice laughed. "Animals in Australia sure have strange names!"

The flight attendant moved farther down the aisle. Dr. Bender undid his seat belt. He stood up and opened the overhead bin. He grabbed his briefcase and began sorting through it.

"Since you're discussing interesting things about Australia," he began, "you should probably have these now."

He handed each intern a book. The books were all the same, with dark-green covers that had the EcoAware logo on them.

"These are your journals," he explained. "Use them to write down things you observe. The EcoAware board and I will want to know what you learned from this adventure. Your journals will be a good way for us to know what it was like for you to study bilbies. You'll be **tracking** them and observing their behavior. Tell us in your journals what that was like."

---

track – to observe the moving path of something

Grabbing a pen, Janice opened her journal. "I don't know a lot about marsupials," she said, starting to write, but I do know a lot about deserts—even the ones in Australia."

Australian Deserts

by Janice

Australia has five major deserts. The Great Victoria Desert, or GVD, is nearest to where we're going. It is located in southwestern Australia. It spreads from the middle of Western Australia into the central part of South Australia. North and east of the GVD is the Simpson Desert. It is located in Australia's central lowlands. Northeast is the Tanami Desert. Straight north of the GVD are the Gibson Desert and the Great Sandy Desert. Both of those are in Western Australia.

The "fasten seat belts" sign flashed on. The flight attendant announced they would soon be landing in Adelaide (AD uh layd).

"Adelaide is the capital of South Australia," Troy said. He studied a map while the others gazed out the window. "It's by far the biggest city in the state. But where we're going," he added, "it doesn't look like there are very many people at all!"

Before the interns knew it, their plane had landed. Inside the terminal, they passed through customs. There, a woman stamped their passports and said, "Welcome to Australia!"

After they collected their bags, they went outside the terminal. They stood near the doors, looking around for Dr. Woollera.

"He told me he'd meet us here," said Dr. Bender. He checked his watch.

Suddenly, they spotted a man hurrying toward them. He was wearing a long-sleeved shirt, khaki shorts, hiking boots, and a big hat with a broad brim.

"G'day, mates!" he said, stepping up to them. "You must be Dr. Bender and my interns." He took off his hat. He had curly black hair and eyes that were almost as dark.

"Sorry I'm late," he said apologetically. "Bit of trouble with the van. Had to stop and fix it. It's right now, though."

The interns excitedly introduced themselves. Dr. Woollera insisted they all call him Duncan. "Or Dunc, for short!" he said with a wink.

Dr. Bender bade them all farewell. "I'll be back here in a month to pick you up," he said, waving goodbye. "Give my best to the bilbies!"

Ten minutes later, they were sitting in Dr. Woollera's van, driving north. It was a tight squeeze with all their bags. There was a cooler and some of Dr. Woollera's gear, too.

"It's about 600 kilometers to the **reserve**," said Duncan. "The reserve is a huge fenced-in area of land where our bilbies live. It'll be your home for the next month."

Troy was doing a quick calculation in his head. His eyes widened. "Six hundred kilometers! That's almost 400 miles!"

"This is a big country," Duncan replied. "Once you get into the outback, everything is really spread out.

"So get comfortable," he added. "And if anyone's thirsty, feel free to grab a lolly water from the esky."

---

reserve – a tract of land set apart for a particular use or purpose

Confused, the interns looked at each other. Duncan smiled when he saw their expressions. He explained, "There are some sodas in the cooler. In Australia, we have some expressions you might not be familiar with. I'll teach you a few."

Australian Expressions   by Troy

Here are some Australian expressions Duncan taught us on the drive up to the reserve.

Ace! = very good
Brekkie = breakfast
Boot = trunk, back of a vehicle
Come good = to turn out OK
Crook = sick
Esky = cooler
Fair dinkum = true, genuine
Flat out = busy

G'day = hello
Lolly waters = sodas
Mate = friend, buddy
No worries! = no problem
Snags = sausages
Spot on! = exactly right
Sunnies = sunglasses
Too right! = definitely

Adelaide and the coast disappeared behind them. The land quickly leveled out. It turned from green to a flat, dusty-red world of sand and clumps of dry-looking grass. There were a few scattered sand dunes but little else.

"You're in the outback now," Duncan said. "Not many people live out here. But there's lots of sky and sand . . . and space!"

The sun blazed down out of a cloudless blue sky. The air was hot and dry. There wasn't a patch of shade anywhere.

"How hot does it get during the day?" Troy asked Duncan, wiping his sweaty forehead.

"Pretty hot," the scientist replied. "During the summer, it can top 35 degrees Celsius. That's about 95 degrees Fahrenheit."

Janice spoke up. "But like most deserts, it gets a lot cooler at night, right?"

"That's right!" Duncan said. "The temperature can drop down close to freezing at night."

The scientist grinned suddenly. "See the big lake off to your right?" he asked.

The interns stared out across the landscape. They saw nothing but dry sand and grass.

Duncan laughed. "It's out there. There's just no water in it right now. It's one of many salt lakes out here. Most of the time, the lakes are completely dry. There are lots of dry creek beds, too. After a big rainstorm, they fill with water. But soon the water's gone again."

Amy was still staring out where the lake was supposed to be. "There's something out there," she said suddenly.

Troy pulled out his binoculars. "It's . . . it's . . . a whole bunch of kangaroos!" he shouted.

Lakes in South Australia   by Amy
Duncan said the dry lakes in this part of South Australia are actually salt lakes. When it rains, water picks up salt from the soil. The water fills the lake bed. Gradually, all the water evaporates. But the salt gets left behind. It forms a crust on the dry lake bed.

Duncan drove closer. He pulled over to the side of the road and stopped. The interns watched a group of lazy kangaroos resting in the shade.

"Hey, Duncan," Drew began. "Why are the kangaroos so . . . well . . . relaxed?"

Duncan laughed. "They're active at night, so they sleep during the day. These are reds," said Duncan, pointing to the kangaroos. "You'll see both red and gray kangaroos while you're here. And just so you know—a group of them is called a mob."

Looking for animals helped pass the rest of the time. As the road slipped by, the interns spotted several more mobs of sleeping kangaroos.

The sun was dipping toward the horizon by the time they reached the reserve. At the main entrance there were a few small buildings. They formed the field station where scientists and volunteers stayed. Duncan showed the interns their rooms. He introduced them to some of the staff. Then he took them out to show them the fence.

"The reserve covers about 60 square kilometers. That's about 24 square miles," Duncan said. "It's surrounded by this tall fence. The fence is cat-proof, fox-proof, and rabbit-proof."

Duncan gazed out at the setting sun. "A long time ago, when white settlers came to this country, they brought rabbits and foxes with them. They brought cats that turned wild. Those non-native animals multiplied. It wasn't long before there were millions of rabbits, foxes, and cats all over Australia.

"The rabbits ate the plants that small native animals lived on," he continued. "The foxes and cats preyed on the native animals. Quite a few species of native animals became **extinct.**

"Bilbies were once common across much of Australia. The white settlers called them pinkies or rabbit-eared bandicoots. The Aborigines—Australia's native inhabitants—called them *walpajirri* or *ninu.*

"Before we began protecting them," Duncan continued, "bilbies were facing extinction. That means they were about to die out completely. There were just a few small, scattered groups of them left in Australia. Fortunately, people got serious about saving them. The National Recovery Plan for bilbies was created. It made

extinct - no longer existing

bilbies a protected species throughout Australia. Zoos and other places started raising bilbies in **captivity.** Gradually, their numbers increased."

Duncan smiled. "Now, bilbies are being reintroduced into places like the reserve. The cats, foxes, and rabbits can't get inside the fence, so the bilbies are safe. They can live and reproduce like they once did long ago. Maybe someday we'll get rid of all the rabbits and foxes in Australia and we won't need fences. But until then, places such as the reserve are the bilbies' best hope for survival."

The scientist looked intently at the interns. "For the next few weeks, you'll be helping me track the bilbies here in the reserve. You'll record information about everything they do—where their burrows are, what they're eating, and other things like that."

The sun had set. It was quickly getting dark. Duncan pulled a flashlight out of his pocket and turned to the interns. "Are you guys ready to meet a bilby?" he asked.

"Absolutely!" exclaimed Drew.

------

captivity - the state of being kept within a certain area

The scientist led them along a trail that ran out into the reserve. After about twenty minutes, he stopped. He pointed to a big clump of grass.

"There's a bilby living near that spinifex grass," he said. "Bilbies are nocturnal, like the kangaroos you saw. They sleep in their burrows during the day. They come out at night to look for food.

"Let's wait quietly and see if it appears," he said. "Bilbies are shy. If we spot one, look fast. It won't hang around for long."

Soon, it was very dark. Overhead, stars were twinkling in the inky-black sky. The interns heard soft scratching sounds coming out of the darkness ahead of them.

Duncan suddenly flicked on his flashlight. "There's your bilby," he whispered quietly.

Crouched beside the clump of spinifex was a small animal with gray fur. It had very long, upright ears and a pointy nose.

The bilby blinked in the bright light. It rose up on its hind legs. Its long ears turned toward Duncan and the interns, who were crouched in the sand. The bilby's nose twitched. Then, in the blink of an eye, it turned and disappeared down into its underground burrow.

"Wow!" exclaimed Drew. He pulled out his notebook and began scribbling down everything he could remember from what Duncan had told them about bilbies.

Bilby Information   by Drew

The bilbies being reintroduced into the reserve are called greater bilbies. Their scientific name is Macrotis lagotis. There was another species of bilby, called the lesser bilby (Macrotis leucura). But it went extinct before people could try to save it. Over the past 200 years, nearly half of the world's mammal species that have died out, or become extinct, have been from Australia.

Bush Tracking

Troy joined the others at the table in the small kitchen of the field station. Duncan had laid out a breakfast of toast and marmalade.

"I can't seem to wake up," Troy said with a yawn. "I must have jet lag. I feel like I could sleep all day."

"Like the bilbies?" Drew teased, giving him a poke in the ribs.

Duncan stirred some milk into his tea. "Sorry, Troy. This is no time for sleeping. While you eat brekkie, I'm going to teach you everything you need to know about bilbies."

While they ate, Duncan talked. Between bites, the interns took notes in their journals.

"The bilby we spotted last night was a male," he began. "Male bilbies weigh from two to about five and a half pounds. Females are smaller. They weigh about two to three pounds."

Duncan took a swig of his tea. "Bilbies usually live by themselves or in pairs. Sometimes you'll see a mother bilby with one or two young ones who aren't quite ready to be on their own yet.

"Out in the reserve, you'll be seeing lots of bilby burrows. Bilbies are really good at digging," Duncan went on. "They dig with their front legs. A single bilby can make up to twelve burrows. None of these burrows are connected. Each one has just a single entrance. In other words, the way in is also the way out."

"What happens if the entrance gets closed off while the bilby is inside?" Amy asked. "How would it get out?"

"Good question, Amy. The bilby would have to clear out the opening. Or dig a completely new exit," Duncan replied.

Troy had stopped eating. He had a puzzled look on his face. "Wait a minute . . . " he said slowly. "Both male and female bilbies dig burrows, right?"

"Right," Duncan replied.

"So how do female bilbies keep their pouches from filling up with dirt while they dig?"

Duncan smiled. "Another good question! The answer is that a bilby's pouch doesn't open at the top, like a kangaroo's. It opens at the back. It's an **adaptation** to keep dirt out of the pouch when a mother bilby is digging."

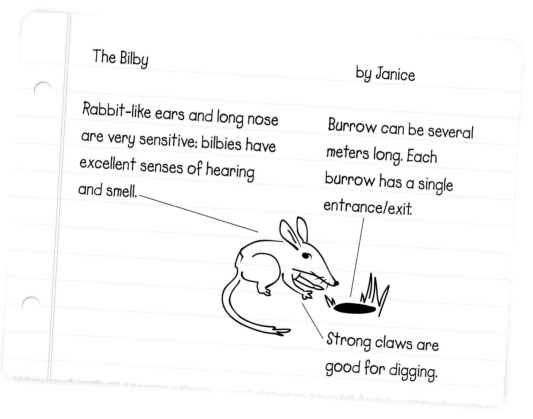

The Bilby

by Janice

Rabbit-like ears and long nose are very sensitive; bilbies have excellent senses of hearing and smell.

Burrow can be several meters long. Each burrow has a single entrance/exit.

Strong claws are good for digging.

adaptation - a change in an animal that helps it live in its environment

Duncan glanced at his watch. He drained his cup. "We need to get to work. Let's meet outside in ten minutes. Be sure to wear your hats. Bring your journals, sunscreen, sunnies, and full water bottles in your packs. We'll be out in the reserve most of the day."

They drove out into the reserve along a dusty track. After a few minutes, Duncan pulled over and stopped the van. He checked their location on a map. Then, with the scientist in the lead, the interns headed out across the dry, dusty landscape.

It was only 8:30 in the morning. But already the air was breathlessly hot. The sun beat down out of a clear blue sky. Heat waves shimmered above the ground.

"Remember to drink lots of water," Duncan reminded them. "The air is so dry that your sweat evaporates almost instantly. So it's easy to get dehydrated very quickly."

"What do animals like bilbies do when they need to drink water?" Amy asked. "I haven't seen water anywhere."

"Most of them don't need to drink," Duncan replied. "They get the water they need from the roots, seeds, insects, and fungi they eat.

"Most of the plants are good at conserving water, too," the scientist added, stopping beside a clump of spinifex.

"That's just like cactus in American deserts," Janice said.

"Spot on, Janice," Duncan said. "Like cactus, these desert grasses are adapted to live in very dry conditions. Spinifex has tough pointed leaves. The plant doesn't lose water easily, even when it's scorching hot. It also has roots that reach far into the soil where there is moisture."

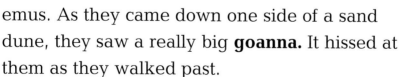

As they continued walking, Duncan pointed out other kinds of desert plants and animals. There were lots of lizards and birds, including emus. As they came down one side of a sand dune, they saw a really big **goanna.** It hissed at them as they walked past.

goanna – a large meat-eating lizard with sharp teeth and claws

At the next dune, they stopped to rest. The fairly flat, dry landscape stretched to the horizon in every direction. There were no houses, no roads—no signs of people anywhere.

Amy turned slowly around. "You know," she said quietly, "it would be really easy to get lost out here."

"Not for most Aborigines," Duncan replied. "They're experts at finding their way through desert country like this." He smiled. "My grandfather was one of the best trackers I knew. He never got lost."

"How about you, Duncan?" Drew asked.

"Naw, I never get lost either, Drew," the scientist said, grinning. "At least not as long as I've got a map and my compass with me!"

They started walking again. After a few minutes, Duncan stopped abruptly.

"Righto! Here we go," the scientist said. He bent down to look at something. "Bilby tracks," he said. "And over there—a burrow."

The interns peered closely at the small tracks in the sand. There were lots of them. A few led to a hole in the ground that was well hidden at the base of a termite mound.

"The first bilbies were introduced into the reserve several years ago," Duncan explained. "Now there are a couple hundred of them. One of our biggest jobs is to keep track of exactly where all the bilbies are living in the reserve."

The scientist pulled a small object out of his shirt pocket.

"That's a GPS!" cried Amy. "I've got one of those. I use it to figure out where I am and where I'm going when I'm camping and hiking way out in the wilderness."

"Nice to have an expert," Duncan said, smiling. "For anyone who doesn't know, GPS stands for *Global Positioning System.* It's a device that uses satellites orbiting Earth to pinpoint the location of something. We use them to determine exactly where all the bilby burrows are."

Duncan pushed several buttons on the GPS. Numbers appeared on the screen indicating their location on Earth. The scientist read out the numbers. The interns recorded them in their journals.

"Just to make sure this is a burrow that a bilby is living in right now, let's look around for other signs of bilby activity," Duncan suggested.

The interns scoured the sand for evidence of bilby activity. They found more tracks and dozens of shallow holes, each a few inches deep, where bilbies had been digging for food. They also found bilby droppings.

Bilby Droppings   by Drew

Bilby droppings look more like clumps of sand than anything else. Duncan said that bilbies eat seeds on the ground by licking them up with their long tongues. The seeds stick to their tongues. But so do lots of sand grains. Bilby droppings can be as much as 90 percent sand!

"Ace!" Duncan exclaimed, after helping the interns record their observations. Then he pulled out a map from his pocket. "We're here," he explained, showing the interns their location on the map. "Let's keep heading west, looking for bilby tracks and burrows. Each time we find some, we'll take a GPS reading. Our goal is to survey this section of the reserve by 11 o'clock. After that, it'll be too hot to work out here."

For the next couple of hours, the interns and Dr. Woollera walked along slowly, scanning the ground for signs of bilbies. Each time they spied tracks or droppings, they stopped. They carefully recorded their position with the GPS and wrote down their observations.

By 10:45, they'd finished their survey. They were dusty, thirsty, and tired. But they were also pleased. They'd located 13 active bilby burrows.

Back at the field station, Duncan made some sandwiches. After lunch, they gathered around Duncan's computer. As the interns read out the GPS locations of the bilby burrows, Duncan entered the information into the computer. When they were done, he pushed a button. A map of the reserve appeared on the computer screen. Each of the thirteen burrows they'd discovered appeared on the map as a small red dot.

"Well done, mates!" Duncan said, looking very pleased. "I think you've really got the hang of bilby tracking!"

Just then, they heard the sound of a vehicle on the gravel outside. A horn honked.

"That's Barry," said Duncan. "Follow me."

A tall man in a broad-brimmed hat was leaning against a truck outside the building.

"G'day, Dunc!" the man called out. "Our little friends are safe and sound in the boot."

The interns followed Duncan around to the back of the truck. He lifted the edge of a tarp that was covering something in the back. The interns peered underneath. From out of the shadows, three pairs of dark, beady eyes stared back at them.

"Bilbies!" cried Janice.

"They're our new arrivals," said Duncan. "They're from a zoo in Western Australia. They were raised there with the goal of releasing them into the wild when they were old enough. It's important to bring new animals into the reserve now and then. They add new genes to the bilby population here."

"New genes?" asked Troy, looking confused. "How do new genes help the bilbies here?"

"I think I know," Amy said. "Genes are found inside cells. They contain information about living things. They control traits such as fur color and ear size. A bilby's genes control everything that makes a bilby . . . well, a bilby."

Janice spoke up. "The genes of one bilby are just a little bit different from those of every other bilby. Putting new bilbies into the reserve brings in new combinations of genes. That adds variety. It's what scientists call genetic diversity. Genetic diversity is a good thing. It helps bilbies survive changes in their surroundings."

Duncan was smiling. "I couldn't have said it better myself, girls."

Then he paused. He looked at the interns. "Would you like to help release these new bilbies into the reserve? We'd need to track them over the next few days. That would mean spending a couple nights camped out in the bush."

Troy spoke up for them all. "Too right," he said with a grin.

A New Home

The interns and Dr. Woollera had spent the morning getting the new bilbies ready to be released. Each bilby now had a small radio transmitter attached to its tail. The transmitter sent out a signal that could be picked up on a special receiver. With it, Duncan and the interns would be able to locate the bilbies wherever they were in the reserve.

"We'll be tracking them for several days," Duncan had explained. "We need to make sure they've dug a burrow, and that they've settled safely into their new home."

After getting the bilbies ready, they packed the van with tents, sleeping bags, and food. They made sure to pack lots of water.

They then set off for the northwestern corner of the reserve. Amy sat up front with Duncan. Drew, Janice, and Troy sat in the back. Each held a bilby in a cage covered with cloth.

The van bounced and lurched along the **rutted** track. A cloud of dust swirled up behind the vehicle. All that could be seen ahead were scattered clumps of grass and red sand.

"Almost there," Duncan said, swerving to avoid a deep rut. "The track ends soon, just before we reach those low dunes."

A few minutes later, the scientist brought the van to a stop. He and Amy helped the others unload the bilbies. They set them gently down in the shade of the vehicle.

"When can we let them go?" Janice asked, peering through a small tear in the cloth covering one of the cages. "I think they'll be glad to get out of their cages."

"We'll release them just before sunset," answered the scientist. "Right now let's set up camp. Then we can explore the area a bit and decide where we want to let the bilbies go."

---

rutted - containing grooves worn into the ground

They set up three tents. Duncan dug a fire pit in the sand. He explained how they'd build a fire in the pit to cook their meals. He also strung up a big tarp next to the fire pit. It created the only real shade for miles.

By 4 p.m., they were ready to go exploring. The sun was slanting down toward the west. The scorching heat of midday was past.

From the top of a dune, they got a good view of the surrounding landscape. "Do you see that dip in the land?" Duncan asked, pointing off in the distance. "That's a dry salt lake. And notice the little gullies that run between the dunes? Those are dry creek beds."

"Duncan, when do you think it rained here last?" Janice asked.

"It's hard to tell," Duncan replied. "A long time ago, I think."

Amy shaded her eyes from the setting sun with her hand. She turned slowly in a circle. "I think this looks like a perfect place to release the bilbies," she announced. "They'll have plenty of plants and seeds to eat around here."

Duncan nodded. "I agree. It looks like a good spot for a new home."

At sunset, the interns carried the cages out to the spot they'd chosen. Duncan tested the radio receiver. He picked up a clear signal from each of the bilbies' radio transmitters.

Drew, Troy, and Janice gently removed the cloths covering the cages. The three bilbies blinked and sniffed the air. Their fur glowed orange in the light from the setting sun.

"Welcome to your new home," Troy said, opening the cage doors.

Two of the bilbies instantly bolted out of their cages. They went bounding across the sand. In seconds, they'd disappeared.

But the third bilby seemed in less of a hurry. Slowly, he hopped out of his cage. He stood up on his hind legs, looking around at his new home. His long nose wiggled as he sniffed the air. He hopped a few feet from the cage and looked back at the scientist and the interns. Then at last he sprinted away as the final rays of sunlight faded from the sky.

Bilby Babies

by Amy

I hope the three new bilbies will settle in quickly and start new lives. Duncan said that bilbies can have up to four litters of babies every year. Female bilbies usually give birth to one or two babies. But some have given birth to as many as four! The babies are only about one-half inch when they're born. They crawl up their mother's body and climb into her pouch. Bilby babies are called "joeys," just like baby kangaroos. They live in their mother's pouch for about 75 days. They drink her milk and grow. Then they spend a couple of weeks in the burrow. After that, they're on their own.

Duncan tested the receiver. "No worries," he said. "I'm picking up all three signals loud and clear. Early tomorrow morning we'll track them. We'll discover how and where they've settled in."

On the way back to camp, Troy almost tripped over an echidna. The top of the little animal's body was completely covered with long, sharp spines. When the interns stepped closer to it for a better view, the echidna rolled itself up into a spiny ball. "That's a pretty cool trick!" Janice said admiringly.

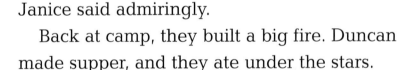

Back at camp, they built a big fire. Duncan made supper, and they ate under the stars.

"We'll have to get up early tomorrow, mates!" Duncan said. "We need to find the bilbies before they return to their burrows for the day."

"Wakie, wakie," Duncan said softly as he woke the interns. It was still dark. But there was a faint rosy glow in the eastern sky.

"We'll have brekkie when we get back," the scientist said. The interns crawled out of their tents. They had their backpacks and journals. Duncan had the receiver and the GPS.

Beep . . . beep . . . beep. They picked up the signal of the first bilby right away. They headed out across the sand. As they got closer to the transmitter—and the bilby wearing it—the signal got stronger. Five minutes later, they spotted the first bilby. She was sitting just outside of a freshly dug burrow at the base of a termite mound. She was lapping up termites with her long tongue. Amy noted the burrow's location on the GPS. Troy wrote down the numbers in his journal. Janice made a little sketch of the site to help her remember where it was.

Duncan changed the setting on the receiver to pick up the signal of the second bilby. They found her at the base of a spinifex clump. She was still hard at work digging her burrow, kicking sand out of the entrance. Once more they recorded the burrow's exact location.

"And now for Number 3," said Duncan. He changed the setting one more time. They listened and waited. But the receiver was silent.

"He might be in his burrow," Duncan said.

"Let's climb a dune," Amy suggested. "We might get better reception."

They turned to a nearby sand dune and began climbing.

Once they were on higher ground, a welcome *beep . . . beep . . . beep* came from the receiver. They followed the signal to a dry creek bed. It ran between two sand dunes. Number 3 had dug his burrow there. They didn't see him, but they were sure he was nearby. The ground was covered with bilby footprints.

The interns and Duncan recorded all the information about Number 3's location. Janice made another sketch, too.

"All three bilbies have settled in just fine!" said Duncan. He sounded pleased. He put away the receiver and finished making some notes. "And now—how about some juicy snags? I'll make some damper, too. It's a sort of bread that can be made over an open fire."

"It all sounds great!" Drew exclaimed, rubbing his stomach. "I'm starving!"

They hurried back to camp, thinking about the food Duncan was going to make. They hardly noticed all the birds that were singing. Or the insects that were buzzing. Or the thorny lizard that scuttled across their path. Or the dark clouds gathering far off on the horizon.

Downpour

Amy woke up to a new sound—*plop . . . plop . . . plop.* It sounded like raindrops hitting the tent. Rain in the desert? Maybe she'd been dreaming.

After breakfast they had all decided to take a nap. None of the interns were used to getting up before dawn. And Duncan's breakfast had been wonderful—and filling!

Amy scooted up to the front of her tent. She unzipped the door and stuck her head out. Heavy clouds were quickly moving across the sky. A warm wind carried the scent of rain.

Plop! Plop! Two big raindrops hit the ground just outside the tent. The drops turned the sand a darker shade of red.

Amy pulled on her boots and crawled out the door. She spied Duncan standing beside the van, looking at the sky.

"Is it really raining?" she asked him.

Duncan nodded, staring up at the darkening sky. "I reckon it is."

Off in the distance, lightning flashed. Several seconds later came the growling roar of thunder.

Drew, Troy, and Janice came scrambling out of their tents. They hurried over to where Duncan and Amy were standing.

"You just might be in for something that's pretty rare here in the outback," Duncan said, still studying the sky. "A fair dinkum rainstorm."

Plop, plop, plop!

Troy turned his face up to the sky. He opened his mouth and tried to catch some of the raindrops on his tongue.

The drops fell faster. The interns danced around in the rain. It felt wonderfully cool. But soon the shower turned into a downpour. Duncan

and the interns ran under the tarp. For several minutes, they stood laughing, watching the rain fall in sheets from the sky.

"Wow, it's really coming down," Drew said with a laugh.

"I hope that the three new bilbies are all snug in their burrows," Amy said, peering out at the rain. "I wouldn't want to be out in this."

But Troy had noticed something. At first the rain had soaked into the sand. But now it was forming small pools in low spots. Tiny streams of water were also flowing across the ground.

The rain went on and on. And the pools and little streams kept getting bigger.

"Once it rained like this back home in Illinois," Troy said. "It rained so much, in such a short time, that the water didn't have time to soak into the ground. We had a flood."

"It's called a flash flood," Janice explained. "Sometimes they happen in Arizona deserts. All the dry creek beds fill . . . with . . . water . . . . " A look of horror crossed her face.

"The bilby!" cried Drew. He understood instantly. "Number 3's burrow was right at the edge of a dry creek bed."

Duncan nodded, frowning. "Yes, it was. And if it's raining as hard over there as it is right here, I'd guess that creek is running with water now."

"But if the rainwater started flooding into the bilby's burrow," Amy interjected, "wouldn't he get out?"

Duncan shook his head sadly. "Not necessarily, Amy. You see, bilbies are very reluctant to come out of their burrows during the day. If the water in the creek rises fast enough, it could flood the bilby's burrow. If the bilby gets trapped inside, it could drown."

For a moment, the interns were silent.

Drew was the first to speak. "We need to go and make sure the bilby is all right. And if he's in trouble, we have to try and save him."

Amy frowned. "But wouldn't that be interfering with nature?"

"I see your point, Amy," Drew said. "But bilbies are really rare. It seems wrong not to do everything possible to help them survive."

"Besides," said Troy earnestly, "this bilby will help add new genes to the population when it reproduces. That's important for the survival of all the bilbies in the reserve."

"And if you think about it," Janice added, "the reserve itself is kind of unnatural. But so was introducing rabbits, foxes, and cats to Australia. The whole point of the reserve is to try to fix what people messed up a long time ago."

Amy nodded in agreement. "OK—I just didn't want us to be doing something we shouldn't."

"That's a good way to be thinking," said Duncan. "Scientists should always consider a problem from every angle. I agree about going out and checking on Number 3. He might be fine. But if he's not, maybe we can help."

Then Duncan called out orders. "Drew, we'll need the two small shovels from the back of the van. Amy, get the GPS, a compass, and the map we made showing Number 3's location. Janice and Troy, pack up the radio receiver. If we can pick up the bilby's signal, we'll know for certain he's left his burrow."

They headed out of camp in the direction of Number 3's burrow. They walked as fast as they could in the pouring rain. But the water had turned the sand into a slimy, slippery mess.

At the top of the first low dune, Duncan and Amy huddled together. Using the map and the

GPS, they figured out exactly where they were and exactly where they needed to go. "It's straight north for about a quarter mile," Amy shouted above the drumming of the rain.

"Then we turn west," Duncan added. "It's a three-minute walk at most."

They slogged on. It was hard going. They kept slipping and falling in the shifting wet sand.

At last they reached what had been a dry creek bed just hours before. Now ankle-deep water was surging down and into the entrance of the bilby's burrow.

"Oh no!" Duncan shouted. "Drew! Try the receiver! Can you get a signal?"

Drew flipped a switch. He held the instrument up to his ear. There was no signal. Looking grim, he shook his head. They had to assume that bilby Number 3 was still inside its burrow.

Slipping and sliding, they scrambled down toward the burrow. Duncan stepped right into the flowing water. The current was strong, but not dangerous. "Hang on to each other!" he called back to the interns. "Take it slow!"

Carefully, the five of them waded through the water. They crowded around the bilby's burrow.

Water was streaming down into the hole even faster than before.

Duncan and Janice grabbed the shovels and started digging. But Troy stopped them, shaking his head.

"It's no use digging, not until we stop the water from flowing in," he cried.

"How do we do that?" Amy asked frantically, staring at the steadily rising creek.

"We have to make a dam! It will keep the water from going down the hole!" he answered. "That's what people do when rivers back home flood. They build dams with sandbags."

With Troy directing, Duncan and Janice shoveled sand as fast as they could, creating a pile in front of the burrow. At first, most of the sand just washed away. But eventually there was enough to resist the flow.

"It's working!" Amy shouted. She and Drew were pushing and piling sand onto the dam with their hands. Gradually, the sand barrier got higher and higher. Finally, it was high enough. No more water was flowing into the burrow.

"Hurry!" Janice urged as Duncan and Drew began shoveling out the burrow. After they'd dug

down several feet, they dropped the shovels and started using their hands. They didn't want to risk hitting the bilby with the shovel.

They kept digging deeper into the waterlogged burrow. Drew reached in as far as he could. His hand touched something soft.

"I feel him!" he cried. Frantically, they all helped push away more sand and water.

"There he is," Duncan said softly. He reached forward and gently pulled the bilby free.

The scientist stood up, cradling the little animal in his hands. The bilby's whiskers and fur were plastered with mud and sand. His eyes were closed. He wasn't moving at all.

CHAPTER 5

After the Flood

Duncan wiped sandy mud out of the bilby's nose and mouth. Very gently, he pressed on the bilby's belly. Water trickled out of the little animal's mouth.

"Come on, mate," Duncan said hoarsely. He lifted the bilby and put his ear to the animal's side.

"Is he . . . dead?" asked Janice hesitantly, not wanting to say the word.

"No," Duncan replied, gently massaging the limp animal. "His heart's still beating. But it's faint. He's very crook. Let's get him back to camp."

Together, he and the interns slogged back through the creek. Duncan gently cradled the bilby. They struggled back across the soggy, slippery sand. All the while, the rain kept pouring down.

Thoroughly soaked, they stumbled back into camp and under the tarp. Duncan laid the bilby down on top of the crate they'd been using for a table. He bent down to listen to the bilby's heartbeat again.

"His heart's beating, and he's breathing," he said. "But he's really cold. Amy, can you get some towels? We've got to get this little bloke dried off and warm."

Amy hurried toward her tent. Seconds later, she reappeared with two soft towels. She slipped the transmitter off the bilby's tail. Then she and Drew gently dried and cleaned the bilby's fur as best they could.

Troy and Janice got one of the bilby cages from the van. With some clean, dry cloths, they made a soft bed inside the cage. Duncan looked closely at the bilby to check its breathing one more time. Then he laid the little animal inside and covered him with another cloth.

"That's about all we can do for now," he said with a sigh.

Drew draped the cage with its canvas cover. Duncan started a fire. "Pass me that billy. I'll make some tea."

"What's a billy?" asked Troy.

"That pot over there," laughed Duncan. "I'll teach you to speak Australian yet."

They sat under the tarp, sipping hot tea. They listened to the rain drumming down. Gradually, the drumming sound began to fade. The rain was letting up. In a few minutes, it had stopped.

The clouds broke up. The sun came out. Sunlight sparkled on the pools of water that had collected around the camp. It shone down on swiftly running creeks. Far in the distance, it shimmered on the surface of a salt lake that had come back to life.

Duncan moved the bilby's cage into the sun. He rolled back the canvas cover and checked the bilby again.

"He's still unconscious," the scientist said. "But he's breathing regularly. He's dry and warm. We've done everything we can. We'll just have to wait and see what happens."

Duncan stood up. "You all go and change into some dry clothes. I'll rustle up something to eat. Believe it or not," he added, glancing at the sky, "the sun's going to set in about an hour. After supper, we should all turn in and get some sleep."

The next morning, Amy, Drew, Janice, and Troy were all up before sunrise. They built a fire and boiled water in the billy for tea. The noise they made woke Duncan. When the scientist crawled out of his tent, he discovered the four interns sitting around the bilby's cage. Janice was writing in her journal.

The Flood

by Janice

Yesterday a flash flood hit around midday. One minute the desert was dry and warm. The next it was flooded with water. The floodwaters poured into the burrow of bilby Number 3, trapping him inside. We worked hard to save him. But this morning we're still waiting to see if he survived.

Duncan poured hot water from the billy into a cup. He dunked a tea bag slowly up and down. "Well, how is our patient?" he finally asked.

"We don't know yet," said Janice, looking worried. "We're all too afraid to look."

Duncan took a sip from his cup and set it down.

"Well," he said, walking over to the cage, "there's only one way to find out."

The scientist carefully lifted one corner of the canvas cover. He peered into the cage.

Duncan turned back toward the interns. He smiled and rolled back the cloth. "Our bilby seems to be better!"

The bilby was sitting up, perky and alert. His fur was dry and fluffy. His eyes were bright.

Drew let out a whoop. "He looks as good as new!" Amy and Troy gave each other a high five. Janice hugged her journal to her chest.

Duncan glanced at the sky. A rosy glow was forming on the eastern horizon. The sun would soon be up.

"Shall we let him go—again?" the scientist asked with a twinkle in his eye.

"Yes," said Troy, speaking for all of them. "Let's do it before dawn. That way he'll have time to dig a new burrow before the sun gets too high and it gets too hot."

The scientist put on a pair of gloves. He gently eased the bilby out of his cage. Then he held him firmly while Drew carefully reattached the transmitter to the bilby's tail.

"All set," said the scientist.

Drew and Amy carried the cage between them. They walked west. The rising sun felt warm on their backs.

They walked for about ten minutes until they finally reached a slight rise in the landscape. The ground here was already drying out. There wasn't a creek bed in sight.

Drew and Amy set the cage down. Troy and Duncan carefully pulled off the canvas cover. Janice knelt down and opened the cage door.

The bilby blinked in the morning light. He stared at the five people for a few seconds. He hopped out of the cage and reared up on his back legs. The bilby's long ears swiveled. His long nose wiggled. Then he sprinted away.

"Go, bilby, go!" Troy called after him. "But stick to higher ground this time!"

"He's going to be fine," Duncan said, as they walked back to camp. "We'll track him tonight to find out where his new burrow is."

Drew had been looking at the landscape as they walked. Now as they approached their camp, he suddenly stopped. "Hey! Does the desert look different? Or am I just imagining things?"

"You're right, Drew," agreed Troy. "It *does* look different."

"There are splashes of green everywhere," said Amy. "Look—there are some right here." She pointed at a cluster of tiny green shoots poking up out of the sand a few feet away. "Those weren't there yesterday."

"Well, in a way they were," Duncan replied. "But yesterday they were seeds or roots. And in a few days, many of the plants that are springing up will be blooming. The rain has brought them to life. Every single drop of rain helps the desert survive."

Janice had brought her journal along. She suddenly opened it and started writing. "Every single drop of rain helps the desert survive," she said softly to herself as she wrote.

"What's up, Janice?" asked Amy.

"Duncan's words made me think of something very important," she replied. "I didn't want to forget them."

"So what's the important thing?" Drew asked.

"When we first arrived in the outback, I was pretty discouraged," Janice began. "It seemed like such a huge job—trying to reintroduce bilbies in a place where they'd gone extinct. Yet all the stuff we were doing seemed to be pretty small. You know, like looking for tracks, and making maps of burrow locations, even releasing the three new bilbies into the desert. Those jobs just didn't seem that important. Like 'drops in a bucket,' as the saying goes."

She paused and looked at her friends. "But maybe those little jobs are more like raindrops in the desert. Maybe everything we do—no matter how small—will help the bilbies survive."

"You're right, Janice," Duncan said. "All the things you're doing for bilbies out here in the outback are important."

He turned back toward the camp. "So let's get going, shall we?" he said. "This adventure has come good. And we've got lots to do."

Report to Dr. Bender

Imagine that Dr. Bender has asked you to write a one-page report about what you have learned about the environment and animals of the outback.

- Draw a cause-and-effect chart like the one below.

- Think about the causes and effects in the story. A cause is the reason something happens. An effect is the result, or what happens next.

- Look at the chart below for a sample.

- Fill in your chart with causes and effects that have to do with the environment and animals of the outback.

- Choose two cause-and-effect relationships from your chart and discuss them in a one-page report.

CAUSE	EFFECT
1. People brought rabbits, foxes, and cats to Australia from other places.	1. The new animals killed bilbies. Bilbies are now extinct in many areas.

Read More About the Australian Outback

Find and read more books about the Australian outback. As you read, think about these questions. They will help you understand more about this topic.

- What are some of the animals that live in the outback?

- What is life like for people who live in Adelaide?

- What is life like for people who live in the outback?

- How do scientists help endangered species in the area?

SUGGESTED READING
Reading Expeditions
Life Science: Ecosystems